A
Chance
to
Grow

For Haven
and new baby.
With Love
Zulema

A Chance to Grow

by **E. Sandy Powell**

illustrations by
Zulma Davila

A BOOK ABOUT
HOMELESSNESS

CAROLRHODA BOOKS
MINNEAPOLIS, MINNESOTA USA

This book is available in two editions:
Library binding by Carolrhoda Books, Inc.
Soft cover by First Avenue Editions
241 First Avenue North
Minneapolis, Minnesota 55401

Library of Congress Cataloging-in-Publication Data
Powell, E. Sandy.
   A chance to grow / by E. Sandy Powell ; illustrations by Zulma
Davila.
      p.   cm.
   Summary: When Joe, his sister Gracey, and their mother are
evicted from their apartment and left homeless, they live in
shelters and on the streets, looking for work and a permanent
home.
   ISBN 0-87614-741-4
   ISBN 0-87614-580-2 (pbk.)
   [1. Homeless persons—Fiction. 2. Dwellings—Fiction.]
I. Davila, Zulma, ill. II. Title.
PZ7.P87715Ch   1992
[Fic]—dc20   91-39678
                                                                   CIP
                                                                    AC

Manufactured in the United States of America

1 2 3 4 5 6 7 8 9 10 01 00 99 98 97 96 95 94 93 92

To Gisela, Willie, Elizabeth
and the man who some people call
Martin
—E.S.P.

To my son, Franz,
and to all single parents
for their strength and courage
—Z.D.

Mama always grew mint outside our back door. I'd sit on the porch steps and pinch the leaves for my baby sister to smell. Sometimes on Saturdays Mama would pull weeds. Then she'd tell us stories of growing up at her grandpa's, and how she helped him with their vegetable patch. Mama wanted us to have a big garden too. But there wasn't room in our housing complex.

Our corner neighbors used to grow tall, blue flowers. But those neighbors moved away. Nobody else seemed to care about growing things. There got to be broken glass on the corner, and old cars with flat tires were left out back.

Mama planted more herbs to cover the alleyway garbage smells.

After school I usually picked Gracey up from the sitter's. Mama worried about us being alone before she got home. She worried more since dad went away. But he had left before Gracey was born. He'd never been home much anyway, so I didn't see what difference it made. But Mama was scared of the neighbors' fights, especially at night.

One morning Mama said, "I'm getting us out of here!" So she got a paper route after her day job. I'd toss papers while Mama drove the van. Baby Grace was happy just coming along. I loved working with Mama! While we drove she'd make up picture-songs about moving to a farm far away from the city. We saved every bit of that route money. Mama wanted plenty for emergencies.

Then all of a sudden we got an eviction notice that said we had to move out in two weeks. We should have been given more time, but the landlord was in a hurry to put up condominiums. I didn't think we had enough money saved, but Mama said, "We'll make do."

With Mama, "making do" was fun. We decorated bags to pack all our things in. She even dug up a few of our herbs for me to take to the country.

Soon we were ready to leave. Mama doesn't like traffic or road signs or finding the right exits, so we drove for hours on regular streets. I tried to keep Gracey happy, but she wouldn't stop fussing. Finally Mama had to turn onto a freeway. Sure enough, right away we were on an overpass jammed with cars. It started to pour. I could see Mama's hands shaking. The wipers screeched. Mama screamed at us to be quiet.

Mama took the next exit just to get us off the freeway. We ended up in a spooky place with huge warehouses and dead-looking streets. Mama needed directions, so we drove around until we found a diner. She parked on a hill, and we went inside. But Mama must have forgotten to set the brake. Somebody in the diner yelled. "Hey lady, isn't that your van?"

We ran outside. I couldn't believe it. Our van had rolled down the hill and smashed into a pole. "It's okay," Mama pretended. "We'll make do somehow." But Mama's face was white. I knew she had hoped to put up the van for our rent deposit. The men said it was "totaled." At least the owner of the diner offered to have it towed away. She even told us to come back if we needed help. Mama packed up the stroller, and I got our garden box.

My mama amazes me. We moved into a hotel and the very next day, she got us a job. Throwing newspapers with a stroller is way harder than with a van, though, and Gracey didn't like coming along anymore. Mama said we were lucky to get that paper job. I didn't see how Mama could feel lucky when our van had just crashed.

Then Grace got sick, so we had to quit. Mama wouldn't let me do the route by myself. I love my baby sister, but sometimes she makes things so hard!

We couldn't afford to keep staying at the hotel, even though it was cheap. Mama heard about a free shelter, so when Grace got better, we decided to go there—just for one night. To save money, we walked the 40 blocks to the shelter. I was hot and achy, but I was proud of us too.

Then at the shelter we had to wait in long lines for Mama to fill out forms. I felt so cramped up I thought I would scream. And some yucky smell was stuck in my nose. Finally the lady at the desk said, "Bed 64. But come back in an hour to meet with your case manager."

Mama didn't look like she knew what she was doing. So I led us through a room with empty tables, to another room full of beds. We followed the numbers to 64. I wanted to lie down even though the bed looked strange, all covered with plastic. But Mama made us wash up first. And because a man kept yelling and staring, she made me go in the ladies restroom with her and then back to wait in line again.

When it was our turn, the case manager asked a whole bunch of questions. She told us we'd be notified when a temporary apartment opened up. But Mama stopped smiling when the case manager said that I really needed to be in school. Mama had told me that if the people at school knew we didn't have a place to live, they might take me away from her. "Joe's way ahead in his class," Mama bragged. "I'll enroll him in school just as soon as we get settled."

"All right for now, until you find a job. Come see me this time tomorrow." And she turned to the line of people behind us. "Next, please!"

At least Gracey fell asleep right away when we got back to our bed. Mama and I couldn't, with all the coughing and snoring. We ended up coming back to the shelter, though, night after night.

Every evening we waited in line. And every evening the case manager asked questions. But there were never any apartments available.

In the daytime, we looked for a job, but Mama couldn't find a place to work where we could all stay together. We mostly just walked. But at least my garden had a chance to grow. The mint had died, but we still had some thyme. Mama said we'd dig wild mint in the country. I didn't know how Mama planned to do that, but I liked thinking about it.

One day a substitute case manager told Mama about an opening at a temporary housing apartment. I was glad because I wanted friends again. Mama hadn't let me talk to street kids. (Lots of them sold drugs, even kids my age.) We got on a crosstown bus and walked a long way. When we finally got there, we saw that the housing units were all boarded up. By the time we got back to our shelter, a sign out front said "FULL." Mama was mad! She asked for the substitute case manager, but she had already gone home.

Mama took us to a Laundromat. It was warm by the dryers. We had eaten a hot dog, but I was still hungry. Mama got me a gumball. We couldn't buy anything else because we had to save money for diapers.

At midnight the Laundromat closed. Mama pushed Gracey and me to an apartment building by the shelter. Since she was nervous that somebody might report us, we went around back. I was really scared. We had to stand guard for each other to go to the bathroom behind a dumpster.

Then we pulled Gracey's stroller right up next to us on the back steps. I was scared of what might come out of the darkness. Mama promised to keep watch all night, but I think she just cried and cried. She must've slept some though, because when I woke up first there was a plate of muffins outside the back door. I can still see Mama biting her lip so she wouldn't start crying again.

Mama didn't act like herself that day. "Just let me think, Joe! Just let me think."

We walked and walked, and finally Mama led us down an alley to the back of a little restaurant. Mama whispered for me to push the stroller out to the street and wait for her there. I was scared, but I did what she said.

Pretty soon Mama came running. She took hold of the stroller and pushed it so fast I had to run to keep up. When we got a block away, I noticed the broom she had shoved in by our bags. "Mama! That's stealing!"

"Joe, I know." She looked away. "We're lucky I didn't get caught."

Mama wouldn't talk to me about the broom. But each morning when we left the shelter, Mama made it her job to sweep out in front and around the old apartment building. It was my job to watch Grace.

Sometimes we found cookies or apples on the muffin steps. We were happy to have any bit of food since we only ate at the shelter kitchen, and the shelter was closed all day. Mama saved us her roll each morning, but my stomach still hurt most of the time. Mama said she absolutely refused to search through garbage like some people living on the streets.

We saw so many street people sitting on benches, and even sleeping right on the sidewalks that I started to feel all mixed-up inside. Regular people didn't seem to see them. Mama tried to keep us tidied up so nobody would think we were homeless too.

It bothered me that my sneakers were full of holes. Mama kept checking at the shelter for newer ones. Sometimes people donated clothes there.

One day I was joking with Gracey and I sort of made fun of a man. I told her he was a bum. Mama stopped me right on the spot.

"Joe, don't ever think you're so smart or so good that you're above somebody else's pain! You can't know what he's been through, not until you know him like you know your own sister." I thought a lot about what she said.

As we walked, Mama looked really tired. We sat down on a park bench. I held Mama's hand. "Joe, I'm sorry about the broom," Mama sniffed. "It was the only way I could think of to give a little back. I hate needing a free bed and food."

"It's all right," I said. But I really wasn't sure.

The next morning Gracey stayed in the stroller while Mama did her sweeping. I was jumping around trying to make Gracey laugh, but she just sat real still. That's when I spotted a sign in the back apartment window.

"Wanted. Cleaning, sweeping, gardening, in exchange for a one-room flat. Ask at Apartment 109."

"Mama, look!"

Mama rushed us right up the steps, carrying Gracey in one arm and the stroller in the other. I knocked at 109. A girl about my age was looking through a peephole. "Oh, hi!" she said. "Just a minute."

Finally a man opened the door. "I'm sorry," he said. "My daughter put up the sign."

"Oh," Mama sighed. I got a big lump in my throat as she turned us to leave.

"But wait," the father said. "There is a room off the laundry. Years ago it was used by a full-time janitor. Come on. I'll show you."

We followed the man and his daughter down the hall and down a couple of steps to a small room. The lump in my throat moved to my stomach and started skipping around.

"It's not much," he said, "but I'll talk to the owner if you like. That is, until you find something better. You come with such a good recommendation!" And he winked at the girl.

I let out my breath when Mama set Gracey down. "Joe," Mama looked at me, "would you mind awfully staying here this winter? We'll get Gracey to feeling better, and then head out to the country come spring."

"All right!" I hollered. I didn't mean to, but I bammed down my garden box so hard on the window ledge that the blind flew up and flapped around. Gracey laughed for the first time in days.

About the Author

E. Sandy Powell lives in a little house in Camas, Washington, on property she and her children call *Sunnyside II*. Their experiences as a single-parent family helped Ms. Powell write *A Chance to Grow*. She worked for fifteen years in teaching and child care. Now Ms. Powell divides her time between freelance writing, parenting, and providing a helping-hand service for senior citizens.

About the Artist

Zulma Davila was born in Cajey, Puerto Rico. When she was seven years old she moved to New York City, where she studied art and graduated from the School of Visual Arts. Now Ms. Davila is a single parent, living in Minneapolis, Minnesota. She wanted to do what she loved the most— to draw—and she wanted to be available for her son, so Ms. Davila started her own business. She and her son love drawing together and they particularly enjoy watching old Errol Flynn movies.